Coast to Coast
In the time of Covid
Stephen Platt

www.leveretpublishing.com

Coast to Coast: In the time of Covid
First published - July 2021
Published by Leveret Publishing
56 Covent Garden, Cambridge, CB1 2HR, UK

The Face Stone, Urra Moor

ISBN 978-1-912460-49-6

© Stephen Platt 2021

All rights reserved. No part of this publication may be reproduced, stored in a retrieval system or transmitted in any form by any means, electronic, mechanical, photocopying, recording or otherwise, except brief extracts for the purpose of review, without the written permission of the publisher.

Coast to Coast
In the time of Covid

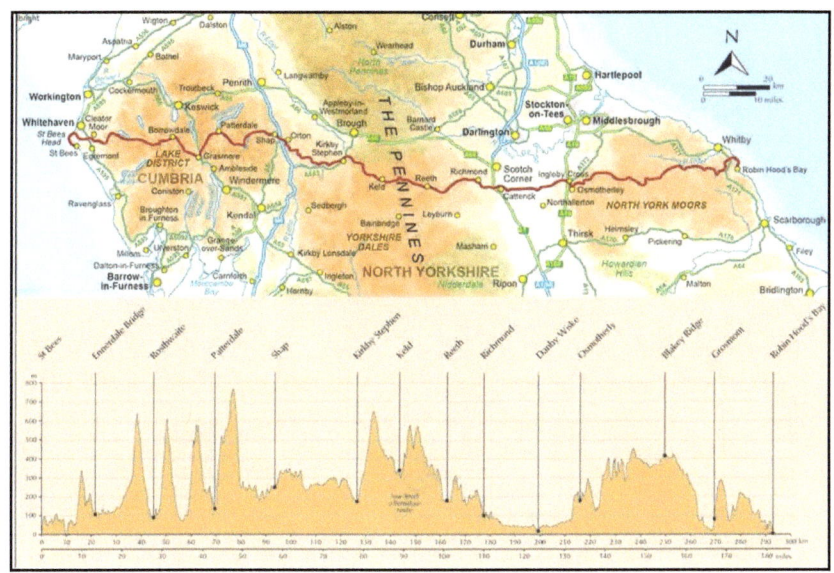

Coast to Coast West

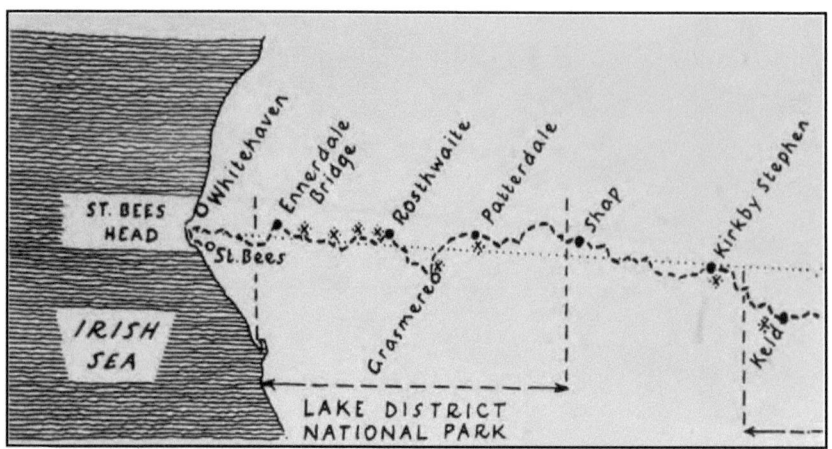

To St Bees Head via Fallowfield, Manchester

Wednesday 19 May 2021

We had arranged to meet Phoebe in Platt Fields, the park opposite the Manchester University Owens campus, where she's been this year. We arrived at the tail end of a thunderstorm and the ducks were swimming on the paths. We had an hour or so to kill before lunch so we set off to walk round the campus as the rain had stopped. Little Court, where I'd spent my first year at University in 1964, has been condemned and has much of the Brave New World architecture that was brand-new then. The campus is much bigger now and attractive with mature planting and big trees. We still had time so we set off on a nostalgia trip to visit Burton Road, where I used to live, and the forge where I used to take Jon and Frances when they were little. I had discovered that the farrier was Jack Priddy. He must have been in his early 60s then. It seems he was still shoeing police horses until a couple of weeks before he died at 96. The Forge had been in his family since the 1700s. It's now been

Scafell and Dunnerdale Fells from Duddon Bridge to Ravenglass road

converted to flats.

The drive up to the Lakes was beautifully sunny and it was hard to imagine tomorrow's awful weather forecast. At Duddon Bridge we turned right and took the single-track road over the moors rather than the coast road. Bright blue sky and low-lying cotton wool cumulus clouds cast great shadows over the hills, and there were fine views of Great Gable and Scafell, Dow Crag and Coniston Old Man.

Moreclose B&B is bright and comfortable and Scharlie slept while I went for fish and chips from Frasier's in the Egremont. We ate them at the dining table with a pot of tea.

Dipping my feet in the Irish Sea at St Bees Head at the start of the walk

Day 1 St Bees to Ennerdale Bridge

Thursday 20 May 2021 (14.0 miles)

I woke early and showered and made tea. I could only manage half the cooked breakfast delicious though it was. Scharlie finished hers alright. St Bees looked delightful and we would have liked to have stopped longer and explore, but I'm nervous and need to get going. At the beach I togged up in my wet weather gear and we strolled down to the beach together to dip my toes in the Irish Sea and to get a pebble to carry across country. Scharlie picked one for me and some for herself.

We posed for photos and I set off to climb the cliff path. A man coming down said, keep going, only another 180 miles to go". I grinned, or grimaced, too intent on the climb to think of a rejoinder. At the top of the slope I looked back and could just make out Scharlie heading back to the car and we waved at each other. A line of breakwaters, a sandy beach beyond the pebbles and the tide going out still. I took a deep draft of the sea air, remarking to myself how much I miss the sea living so far inland.

Line of breakwaters at South Head. Scharlie walking back to the car and waving

The cliffs here are red sandstone, home to nesting sea birds – thuggish herring gulls, jackdaws tumbling in the gale, kittiwakes scything through the air on elegant scimitar wings, black cormorants soaring high along the length of the cliffs and guillemots hugging the waves and heading out to sea in search of food. Birds on the ledges and on the grassy tops of the cliffs, safely separated from the main edge. But not as many as I would have expected. Carpets of pink thrift on the south facing slope of an inlet and white sea campion on the opposite north facing slope.

I passed the lighthouse and caught up with two women, Alison and Judy who were also doing the Coast-to-Coast. They live in Cambridgeshire and although this is their first big walk they had been training since February. I learn later that their husbands are acting as a support crew in two campervans when the man I'd seen at the start of the walk turned out to be one of the husbands. Just before Cleator, near the Wainright statue, the women piled into their respective vans to change out of their wet clothes. I wasn't that wet, having started out from St Bees in my wet weather gear.

I followed the cycle trail rather than walk on the road and in Cleator I bought a meat and potato pie at the post office village shop for a late lunch and went back to eat it in the porch of St Leonard's Church in Cleator. I've

Fleshwick Bay, half way along the Head, pink thrift and white sea campion

eaten half and the rest is under my fleece keeping warm. I checked my phone and couldn't believe I'd only done 6 miles; I was already tired and sore. The pull up Dent starts on a forest track. I'm going slow, plodding along and I stopped to rest on a pile of logs. The final grassy slope of Dent would have seemed easy a while ago. Today, with a pack, trying to stay upright in the teeth of a gale, it is tough. Its only 352 metres, about the same as Leveret Croft, but it seems more because Cleator is only about 90 metres above sea level. I stopped again for a minute or so on the top in the lee of a cairn. No long rests today, too wet and windy.

From the summit it's a steep descent down the grassy slope of Raven Crag and into the beautiful Nannycatchgate Valley. This would be a good place to camp in better weather alongside the fast flowing stream on a soft grassy bank. A strange whistling and then a large herd of horses driven by a man on a quad bike passed me heading into the narrow valley and its lush grazing. I feel slow and tired and saw a pair of boot prints in the mud – maybe the two women got ahead of me on the Moor Row to Cleator stretch when I took the alternative path along the national bike trail. Finally I descend into Ennerdale Bridge along a high footpath parallel to the road.

I changed out of my wet gear in the porch of the B&B, found my room and

Delightful Nannycatchgate, Valley and Beck

made tea. My host has booked me into the Fox and Hounds for dinner. The two women from early today were just finishing their drinks. It seems they got in an hour after me so the boot prints were from someone else. They'd seen me on the top of Dent near the cairn, they said, just as they were beginning the climb. They asked if I had found the navigation difficult and I said it seemed pretty clear. They thought it was tricky especially towards the end.

Three strapping young men on the table next to mine were camping. They'd come here because it was even worse in the Rhinogs in Central Wales where they had intended to go. They'd ordered a burger. It arrived like the leaning Tower of Pisa. I asked for a simpler version but it was still daunting and I left half of it. They challenged me to finish. I said at my age I couldn't afford to eat that much.

Fell ponies in Nannycatchgate

Day 2 Ennerdale Bridge to Rosthwaite

Friday 21 May (15.2 miles)

My stomach still rejects food this morning. Maybe it's nerves; I am nervous. Ros, my host, is a big lady with a mass of blonde hair. The breakfast was beautifully cooked – bacon two poached eggs and tomatoes. But all I can eat was one of the eggs. I had a blue funk like this before a big cross-country run when I was a teenager. Let's hope I feel fine later today. It's disorientating staying in a B&B rather than camping and having to brave the elements anew each day rather than feeling part of them.

I feel better as soon as I set off and head off down the road to the lake. The tops are in cloud and the water looks cold. The path on the south side, around Anglers Crag and Robin Hood's Chair, is awash with raging torrents from last night's rain. It meant rock hopping from stone to stone to keep my boots reasonably dry. I passed or was passed by several people and caught up with a young woman and fell into conversation with her. She asked various

Start of south side track round Ennerdale Water

things to see if I knew what I was doing and then tagged along. I fancy she could have walked quicker than me but she clearly valued the company. It was her first big walk. She works as a publisher's agent in London turning novels and memoirs into drama. We talked about Soho. The agency is on Lexington and she said that it had been nicer during lockdown. They close the streets and the restaurants and bars put down Astroturf and marquees, she said. Before lockdown we were expanding. We had taken a lease on an adjacent building that would have needed remodelling and we would have expanded into Shaftesbury Avenue and Noho. Now we've got used to working from home I expect I will only go into the office two days a week. Have you been more or less productive working from home? More, much more; no interruptions. You work when and how you like. But I miss the company.

Yasmin had done her research for the trip. I enjoyed planning when I couldn't get away during lockdown. She had registered with one of the tour companies who booked the accommodation and carried her suitcase. My suitcase is huge and I filled another bag with books. I don't get a chance to read all year, I'm too busy reading for work. Yasmin read English at Cambridge and had friends in architecture. I told her about my travels for the disaster recovery research and about doing the Pennine Way last year. She said she liked reading other

Yasmin eating lunch in the rain outside atmospheric Black Sail YHA

people's accounts of their trips and I told her about my blog.

We had to stay on the south side of the river because they're logging on the other road. The sky had cleared a little and we could now see all the way up Tongue Beck leading to Windy Gap and Green Gable. Richard, Scharlie's son, warned me not to carry on up this obvious path but to bear left up the hillside to Grey Knotts. I can imagine where it goes to the lowest point on the ridge; it looks fairly steep. To our right the black cliffs of Pillar Rock against the skyline.

Just after we passed the Black Sail Hut, on the other side of the river, we came to a log bridge with an overhead cable. Is this it, asked Yasmin. Let's try, I said, and ventured out along the log. But the log stopped at a vertical post some 2 metres from the opposite bank and a mesh fence filled the gap. I launched across, trusting the mesh wouldn't break and drop me into the river. There was a heart stopping moment when the lathe at the bottom of the fence that I was standing on broke off. Luckily my boots were through the mesh and I managed to hang on and reach the bank. Like Tarzan, said Yasmin, looking doubtful and trepid as she climbed up onto the log and started across. This is not a good idea, I was thinking, then looking upstream I spotted a footbridge a few hundred yards away and shouted to her that she should walk on. She looked most relieved. I had to wade across a bog to reach the main

Brandreth Hause below Grey Knotts. North to Haystacks, Buttermere and Crummock Water

Slate quarry buildings at Honister Pass

Seatoller, at the foot of Honister Pass. Wettest inhabited place in UK (3.55m / annum)

path and return to the hut where we agreed to meet and have lunch. What possessed me, I wondered. Wish I'd thought to get her to film it! The hut was all barred and shuttered so we sat outside in the rain and ate our sandwiches.

Leaving the hut we followed an indefinite path and reached the well-made path next to Loft Beck that climbs steeply up to below Haystacks. The path is well made with stones that make a staircase. We took it slowly and finally reached the ridge. Looking back towards Fleetwith Pike and Haystacks we can see Butermere and Crummock water. There is a bit of a slog across the cairned moor top to the old tramway of Moses Trod that descends all the way to the main quarry buildings of Honister Pass. Outside there is a pretty green narrow-gauge quarry steam engine. We stopped for tea and a loo break and then made our way gently down to Seatoller, past the YHA and a field of camping pods that Yasmin says are expensive. On the path through the woods there's a 'bad step' with chains just before Rosthwaite. There was no room where Yasmin was staying, but Anne-Marie, her host, rang round and found me a room at Gillercombe B&B with Rachel Dunckerley. I don't do evening meals any more since my husband died, she said. Can't be bothered. It was a lot of work when people arrived at different times. I still get up early to feed the sheep. I've been all over – Everest, Costa Rica, New Zealand.

Gillercombe B&B (Host Rachel Dunckerley)

Day 3 Rosthwaite to Glenridding

Saturday 22 May 2021 (15 miles)

Since the weather forecast is bad I telephoned round and arranged to stay in a B&B in Glenridding and since I'm not using the camping gear I booked Sherpa Van to pick up my rucksack tomorrow.

A good nights sleep and a more modest breakfast. I was first down and Rachel was ready with coffee and fresh fruit and brought me my two poached eggs with a laugh. She has four great-grandchildren. She's 78 with long thick auburn hair, going grey now, and tied in a thick ponytail. The most striking things about her are her eyes, sparkling and laughing, and a beautiful grey parrot she's had 25 years, that sits on her shoulder which she talks to all the time.

I pack quickly, Rachel found a strong bin bag for my stuff and yellow tape to make it fast and I was away soon after. You know the way, she said, Stonethwaite and over the bridge. Immediately on leaving the house there was a sign and I realised that I didn't need to walk a mile down the road and I could

Rosthwaite looking up Stonethwaite Beck towards Eagle Crag

cut across and join the track up Stonethwaite Beck and Greenup Gill. I was first away, which made me feel good, and I made steady progress on the stony track by the side of the beck with the dark bulk of Eagle Crag looming ahead.

Eagle Crag and diff. rock climb of Corvus

Nearing the top of Stonethwaite Gill

The stream is broad at first and then narrows below Eagle Crag, tumbling in a series of falls. The cliff looks foreboding – black, wet and steep. I can see the route of Corvus that goes across the steep buttress at an easy Diff. standard that I did years ago and pass an ancient knarled holm oak.

I'm going fairly well today, still slow, and it feels good not to have the heavy pack. The path goes on and on, steepening by the side of Long Crag then reaching the ridge of Greenup Edge before swinging due east and climbing to a boggy plateau. An inviting ridge curves away south to the summit of High Raise and on to the steep cliffs of Pavey Ark and the Langdale Pikes. It's a mile or so to the descent down Easdale Gill. I have vague memories of doing this on my first serious camping trip with the scouts when I was about 14. It was a boiling hot day then and we toiled up the path by the side of the gill. I'm impressed by how well we did although I remember at the time being very disappointed by our dismal performance, not least when we got lost on Red Pike, descending into Buttermere rather than following the ridge of High Stile, High Crag and so back to Rosthewaite where we were camped. Our economics teacher came over Honister and rescue us in his vintage Alvis.

Below Helm Crag a tall tree stump with the carving of a barn owl in flight, then the well-appointed stone homes of Landrigg, just north of Grasmere.

Above Greenup Edge looking west to Great End with Scafell Pike in cloud

Easedale Gill and Gibson Knott

Carving of a barn owl below Helm Crag

I stopped under a tree for a short rest, an oat bar and an apple from breakfast. It was spotting with rain but I thought it would hold off. Looking back at the cliffs of Helm Crag I rather wished I'd taken the high route along the Gibson Knot ridge rather than descending the gill. Nevermind, it's a long way still.

There was a mile or so of road to reach the Ambleside-Keswick Road that I cross over and begin the climb up Tongue Gill. It seemed a long way. I remembered how I used to bound up these paths. I did the Fairfield Horseshoe, the mountain immediately to the east, in a couple of hours in my early twenties and was caught out in shirtsleeves in a hailstorm crouching behind a wall on a summer's day, shaking with cold.

I paced myself and went steadily, passing others despite my slow pace. A young man was swimming in Grisedale Tarn. Impressive I said as I passed. His party laughed, stupid more like, they said. Ruthwaite Lodge looked good, but all shut up. Another ten-minute rest and then the long descent of Grisedale Beck, taking the rougher left-hand trail. A man on a quad bike and a dog herding sheep. A tidy farmhouse and neatly stacked bales of hay. I'm slow yet I'm ahead of the young men who have overtaken me but who stop for longer rests while I plod on.

Tongue Gill and path to Grisedale Hause

Grisedale Tarn

Ruthwaite Lodge

Across the stone bridge and into Patterdale. There was a Saturday cricket match in progress and I was tempted by the smell of fish and chips from the mobile chippy. But I slog on along the road to Glenridding, finally reaching Glenridding with its shops and tourists in the late afternoon sunshine. Nemia, my host at the Fairlight B&B, said I'd booked for tomorrow. I said no, it was for today. She said you're lucky there's been a cancellation for a wedding and the king-size room is free but it's £10 more. I didn't argue. I had a shower and changed into clean clothes, having washed my socks and underpants. I bought a bottle of Coniston Bluebird pale ale, a pasty, a tuna and cucumber sandwich and grapes. Nemia kindly heated the pasty for me and I ate in isolated splendour in the dining room.

I'm reading O'Brien and tonight its Desolation Island. I like the ingenious fortitude, it inspires me to deal with the petty hardships of the walk.

Stone bridge Patterdale

Saturday cricket match in Patterdale

Arrival in Glenridding in evening sunshine

Day 4 Glenridding to Shap

Sunday 23 May 2021 (15.6 miles)

I felt lazy this morning and lay abed. Breakfast is at 8 and I have plenty of time to dress and pack. I've rung Sherpa Van again and they will carry my bin bag to Shap. The rain is lashing down outside and the wind is howling and it's another big day with a stiff climb at the start and then on to Kidsty Pike, a long walk along Hawes Water and on to Shap. Luckily it was only drizzling for the walk back along the main road to Patterdale and the start of the track up to Angle Tarn. I had been rather dreading this ascent but it was steady and I didn't find it too bad. I can see Brothers Water and the road up the Kirstone Pass but the tops are in mist. The path levels at Boredale Hause. Various paths cross here, some more obvious than the one I need, and I take a bearing with my compass. Then the complex shapes of Angle Tarn appear in the mist and I know I'm on the right track. I was on my own and it felt wild and isolated, then I spotted someone on the skyline and then a green tent next to the tarn.

Track from Patterdale to Boredale Hause

The wind really picked up and the gale caught my poles and blew them sideways and it was all I could do to stay on my feet. Further on it was so bad I sheltered behind a low wall and as the sky cleared for a moment I watched the shadows of the clouds race across the hillside. The wind disorientates and the rain and mist makes navigation difficult and I carried on up the ridge towards Rest Dodd, thinking I had already reached the slopes of Rampsgill Head and missed the path that contoured right. Rather than go back and retrace my steps I cut right down the steep slope, losing the 200 feet I had climbed up the ridge and regained the path.

I met a man doing the coast-to-coast east to west. He said he done it the other way round last year. He'd come from Shap and must have made a very early start or was moving a lot faster than me. I was feeling isolated again as I neared High Street, then two runners in shorts with bright pink legs ran past and continued up the main drag to High Street summit. I marvelled that I had cycled along the whole ridge from just south of Penrith to Ambleside, the Roman Road from the fort of Brocavvm in the north to Galava in the south, just a couple of years ago. I headed north up Rampsgill Head, contouring below the summit, before curving away east to Kidsty Pike. I could now see the silver thread of Riggindale Beck leading down to Haweswater from where

Angle Tarn appearing out of the mist

The main drag rising to the summit of High Street (828m)

High Street ridge from Rampsgill Head

Kidsty Pike (78m) the highest point on the Coast to Coast

I imagined it would be an easy level walk to Shap. What wishful thinking!

Again it was hard to stay on my feet on the summit of Kidsty Pike and so I had a brief respite behind the half-hearted cairn. The descent is easy at first but begins to steepen and I was just having a pee when a dog appeared. Bet that gave you a fright, the dog's owner said. It's great to get out. I don't mind the weather. My wife is ill and I'm her 24/7 carer. My boy's looking after her today. She's got motor neurone disease. She used to come out walking with me and it's killing her seeing me getting out; I'm doing the Horseshoe, up Kidsty Pike and back down Long Stile and Rough Crag.

The next stretch was surprisingly difficult, scrambling down broken cliffs and I had to take care not to trip. Finally the rock ended in steep grass slopes down to the woods on the lakeshore. I stopped for a quick bite behind a wall – banana and yoghurt from breakfast. I'd imagined it would be plain sailing along the lake, but it was a typical rocky Lakeland path, bouldery with lots of ups and downs. It was raining and I had my hood up. Going down a rocky defile I stumbled and my foot slipped. My poles had no purchase on the slick rock and slid away and I pitched headlong. I was aware of falling in slow motion. Aware of the poles skittering away and trying to protect my head and chest

Haweswater from the lower slopes of Kidsty Howes

Bluebell wood bewteen Burnbanks and Naddle Bridge

and realising they would be fine but also aware of my knee grazing a rock and my thigh landing on a sharp-pointed stone; trying to protect it but feeling it sinking forcibly onto the point of the rock. Scrambling to my feet I flexed my leg to see if it would still work and if I could continue and work off the pain. Realising I couldn't I stopped in the pouring rain to fix a plaster to my bleeding knee and to rub Arnica into my thigh. It was painful walking there was no option but to press on.

Finally, I reached the dam at the end of the lake and began the next stretch through farmland, first through a bluebell wood down to Naddle Bridge, a stone arched bridge sheltering an even more ancient packhorse bridge. Then along the river to Rawhead Farm and a complicated crossing of pastures and boggy gorse moorland until Shap Abbey came in sight. I couldn't find a gap in the tall limestone wall so I climbed over, taking care to find a good place with holds and avoiding dislodging the coping stones. I was very tired by now and it was raining hard and I wondered if I'd make it. Finally along the metal road that led into Shap. The New Ing Lodge is superb – warm and welcoming. I took off my boots in the porch, dumped my pack in my room, relaced my damp boots and set off in search of the chippy. I ate my fish and chips in the dining room of the lodge with a pint of Ullswater pale ale.

Naddle Bridge sheltering the ancient grass-covered pack-horse bridge

Rawhead Farm near Swindale Beck on the way to Shap

Packhorse bridge, Swindale Beck

Abbey Bridge

Shap Abbey (12th Century)

Day 5 Shap to Sunbiggin Tarn

Monday 24 May 2021 (10.7 miles)

The day dawned bright and looked much better. My leg is still painful but good to go. The breakfast slot – because of Covid - was not for an hour, so I had a lazy time reading and packing. My rucksack, which I'd left in the boiler room was dry, although my boots were still damp despite having stuffed them with newspaper and putting them on top of the boiler.

Eeva brought my two fried eggs and we got chatting. She is from Estonia. I asked how the lodge had survived during lockdown and she said without furlough it would have been impossible but they'd managed to get through without losing any staff. She went back to Estonia and was away two months.

I set off down the A6 south, found the path across the fields and climbed the footbridge over the M6. My sore thigh is holding up well but the sack feels heavy now I'm carrying all my gear again. It is supposed to be sunny and dry today but it began to rain so I stopped to put on my rain gear. I had just

Crossing the footbridge over the M6

finished when a woman passed me. I caught up with her a little later when she'd stopped to read the map. She said she was meeting her husband in Orton. He got a lift with Sherpa van today. We're only going as far as Kirby Stephen. We found the Lakes hard and my husband hurt his knee coming down Grisedale Beck. She seemed competent and fit. How did you manage yesterday over High Street in the wind, I asked. We didn't, she said. We caught a ferry from Patterdale to the far end of the lake and crossed to Shap on a lovely low route. I'm 66, she said, and this is the hardest walk we've done. What else have you done, I asked? Offa's Dyke and the West Highland Way, which we liked. We booked again with the same tour company, Macsadventure. They're Scottish and not as well organised down here as they were up there.

She wanted to crack on and not keep her husband waiting in Orton. So when I stopped to strip off the rain gear she shot off. I was debating where to camp that night. I had thought to reach Smardale Bridge, the only river on my map, but it was still a long way.

I stopped for lunch at Orton Crag – banana and half a muesli bar. Just below the crag a spring gushed forth from below a small limestone pavement, so I stopped to fill my bottle which meant I could camp anywhere.

The way traverses east across rich pastures, boggy from heavy rain, with

Limestone pavement Crosby Ravensworth Fell

mud wallows around gates where cattle had stood. I stopped to chat to a farmer who was building a dry-stone wall in front of his farm and asked him the way. Where are you from, he asked. Derbyshire. Like round here although we're on the gritstone. This is limestone, he said, pointing to the stone in the tractor barrow. How many days to go? This is my fifth, so eight more. So nearly halfway. Yes, at Keld.

Finally the farmland ended and I reached Tarn Moor. Curlew calling and a green path through the stunted trees. There was a low crag overlooking the tarn and a flat green space so I pitched camp and lay in the warmth of the evening sun for a while.

Campsite on the edge of Tarn Moor above Sunbiggin Tarn

Day 6 Sunbiggin Tarn to Kirkby Stephen

Tuesday 25 May 2021 (12 miles)

I had a peaceful night despite the hard ground with only an inch of turf over limestone pavement. I woke about four after seven hours good sleep. The curlew continued calling in the night and there was a gentle rumbling of grouse, quite unlike their alarm calls. It rained hard and I dozed till six.

I packed and forced down some muesli to give me energy for the next stage. The rain stopped and I was able to shake off the water and pack tent and set off just before eight.

The route leads over Ravenstonedale Moor on a bridleway. Skylarks singing their hearts out. I felt fairly good and stopped to talk to a small group of men who were waiting for a slowcoach. They were on the last leg of the Dales Way walk and asked me what I was doing. They said it had been rough on Great Whernside but that they had really enjoyed it – better than work at any rate, they said. We were admiring your style climbing the fell – very steady, said

Bridleway across Ravenstonedale Moor

Smardale Bridge and Scandal Beck

Old Smardale viaduct on the abandoned South Durham and Lancashire Union railway

one of them. I felt like saying it's all I can do now, slow and steady, but when I thought about it I realised that my style, when I'm going well, is very economical and I use the poles in sync with my steps. We parted and I continue below Great Ewe Fell and pass Bents Farm that advertises camping. I'm glad I camped where I did at Sunbiigin Tarn since, apart from the campsite at the farm, there was nowhere obvious.

I got slightly lost above Scandal Beck and I went down through an underpass below a disused railway line. I soon found the right path and crossed Smardale Bridge. A farmer on a quad bike was herding sheep with a single dog just like the one I'd seen in Grisedale. Seems to be the style now. Looking back I could see the line of the railway track and the beautiful Smargale Gill viaduct. I wondered where the line used to connect and what labour and expense went into its construction. It seems so incongruous today in this intensely rural setting. I learnt later the line ran from Tebay to Kirkby Stephen and carried stone and other minerals as well as four passenger trains a day. I could see the limestone quarry and could make out the opening of the two lime-kilns just before the viaduct.

Lapwing calling peewit as I slogged up Smardale Fell. I went wrong again on reaching the road, turning left instead of right, trusting my instinct, too lazy to

Lime kilns and associated quarry next to Smalldale railiway line

get out the map. The way drops down through pastures to an underpass on the main Carlisle-Settle line and I just had time to whip out my phone and take a photograph 0f the roaring majestic stream train, vowing to try and book a trip with Scharlie.

At Greenriggs farm I heard the harsh cry of a raptor I thought might be a kestrel. It took off from a tall tree in the wood to my right and as it spread its wings and soared over me I realised it was much bigger with square shaped wings and narrow tail – a Goshawk maybe I thought. It continued to fly back and forth as I walked calling loudly. The mate, the male I presumed, soared much higher away to the north. Looking up and following the flight of the two birds, I missed the path and rather than go back, I cut across a field between gates and rejoined the narrow lane further down. Still no sign of the town, apart from sheds and the floodlit sports ground. Into a housing estate then the main road and the Jolly Farmers guest house. No one home, so into town to the Mulberry Bush cafe. Coffee followed by broccoli and stilton soup, then a pot of tea and coffee and walnut cake.

I rang Scharlie and arranged to meet her tomorrow in Keld and suggested she and Bridget do a short round walk up the Pennine Way. I ordered a second pot of tea when they politely asked me to give up my table and read and

The "Dalesman". Steam train on Settle to Carlisle linenear Kirkby Stephen

wrote till after four o'clock by which time the door of the Jolly Farmers was wide open and Carol greeted me with an offer of tea and scones. I opted for a room with a bath and had a delicious soak, which did wonders for my sore leg.

Over tea I got chatting with a man from Salisbury who comes up to photograph steam trains. He snapped the one I saw today. He swears a lot and is most talkative but I'm feeling benign and encourage him. Then a party of six bikers arrive from Devon, having driven 350 miles. They're all in their 60s and come here every year to rid e the Dales. I wonder if I'm doing the right thing planning to sell my motorbike. Spicy prawns roast lamb and Wainright's ale for dinner then early bed.

Jolly Farmers guest house Kirkby Stephen, (Host Carol Pepper)

Day 7 Kirkby Stephen to Keld

Wednesday 26 May 2021 (12.0 miles)

Breakfast was early and Carol and Sandra were all ready to serve the first meal of the day – fresh fruit followed by smoked haddock and two poached eggs. I'm beginning to develop an early-morning appetite at last! I packed last night and it didn't take me long to get ready. I'm leaving my camping gear in the black sack for Scharlie to pick up this afternoon on her way to Keld. It had been raining hard but looked as though it was clearing and decided to try the winter route and not go all the way to the summit of Nine Standards because of the low cloud and poor visibility and because I'd done it before. Carol wanted me to walk along the road. I checked the room but forgot my poles, noticing as soon as I'd left. Carol let me fetch them in my boots. The motorbike crew and train spotters were up and breakfasting.

I was photographing St Patrick's Church when another solo walker passed

Setting off in the rain from Market Street, Kirkby Stephen

me. I followed him up the road and then overtook him. I'm going well. Finally the paved road gave out and a stony track followed. We entered the cloud and visibility dropped to 50m so I stopped and waited for him and suggested we walked together. He said he wanted to go to the summit. I said I'd see how I felt. In any event it was fairly easy walking, especially chatting. Mark is a GP and head of his practice. He said he'd had a heart attack from stress. I asked him if that had changed his life. He said it had. He'd cut down his hours and is working as a locum and taking time out. I'm not an experienced walker, he said. You seem to be going well. You passed us on the Grasmere to Patterdale section, he said. What happened to your two companions, I asked? One is going with Packhorse and the other wanted to crack on. We were all staying in different places anyway, he said.

In the event I continued with him to the summit. From there it got increasingly boggy and where the path divides we took the August to November path. It was incredibly wet and we had to wade through streams. At one point I went in up to my knee but amazingly my gaiters and over-trousers kept the water out of my boots. We stopped briefly for a bite in Whitsundale Beck and, leading off, I set a cracking pace – the first time I felt I could move well and this pleased Mark as he wanted to get as far as possible today. It's much

John Waller (Royal Navy purser 1810) Cloisters, Market Square, Kirkby Stephen

Mark in thick mist on Nine Standards Rigg (662m)

Tom, Richard and Scharlie on summit of Nine Standards, August 2016

Ravenseat Farm, closed due to Covid restrictions 2021

Cream tea at Ravenseat Farm (home of Yorkshire sheperdess, Amanda Owen) 2016

Whitsundale Beck (blue Autumn Aug-Nov route to Ravenseat)

Oven Mouth, Whitsundale Beck below Ravenseat

harder when the ground is so wet, negotiating bogs and watercourses, very like Kinder. We stopped again at Ravenseat, where Amanda, the Yorkshire shepherdess lives, but its all closed up today, so no tea and scones like we had with Richard and Tom when we did a day with them five years ago. Two walkers, who'd passed us earlier, turned up having come over the summit route, complaining bitterly about the bogs and how they had had to zig-zag about, taking longer than us on a shorter route. I didn't feel so bad with our route choice now. Mark needed to get cracking as he doesn't know where he's stopping tonight. Last time we came this way with Richard and Tom we joined the road but today I took the correct path on the north side of the stream. The Swale is swollen today and looks like Coca-Cola. Delightfully they let me in at Keld Lodge and I was able to rest make tea and shower before Scharlie and Bridget arrived. Dinner at the Lodge was excellent.

Wainwath Force, Birkdale Beck, main tributary of Swale

Coast to Coast East

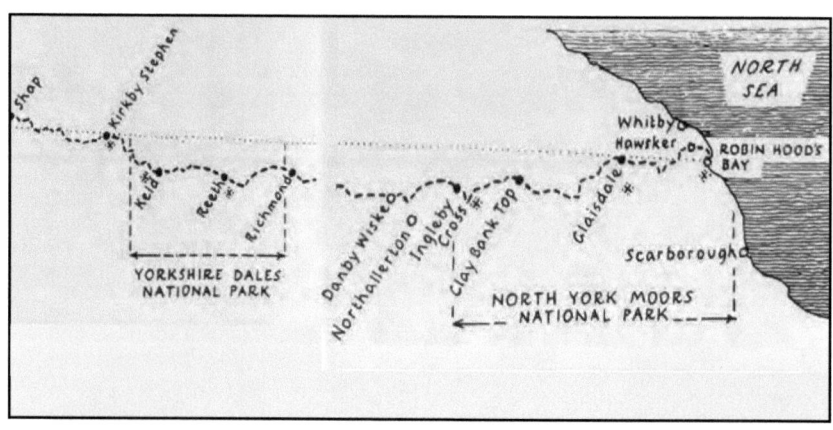

Day 8 Keld to Reeth

Thursday 27 May 2021 (12.2 miles)

A delightful day along Swaledale through woodland paths by the riverside. We breakfasted well and set off in good order soon after nine. The day looked promising with the sun beginning to break up the low cloud. As we left the lodge there was a beautiful mirror image of a lone tree in the distance. The sun was out by the time we reached Catrake Force on East Gill, where I camped when doing the Pennine Way, and we climbed the broad track rising high above the river and contouring round. The path divides here – left onto the moor for the high route which we'd heard was boggy, and right the longer riverside route, which we opted for.

All went well till near Ivelet when climbing the heights Scharlie exclaimed that she'd dropped her cap. I offered to go back and tried my best to hide my annoyance since today was so special for her and she was mortified. Unfortunately, we had just descended quite a way to Gunnerside Beck and

Setting off from Keld Lodge

Mirror image shadows above Keld

East Gill, where I camped on Pennine Way and was woken at midnight by irate farmer

View of River Swale. To the right Kisden Side, Black Hill in the distance

Footbridge over Swimming Gill, tributary of the Swale

High road to Gunnerside

Isles Bridge, Hatter's Roof

have climbed out of it. So retracing our steps was a hot slog. I met a party of people and asked if they'd seen a cap. Yes half a mile back at the top of the rise where it flattens out. Of course it's at the top, I thought. Scharlie said, My hero, on my getting back.

Instead of taking the meadow route which looked a little boring crossing one pasture after another we continued on the high metalled bike trail until Gunnerside. Perhaps because of the mishap with the cap rather than continue along the same high line, which would have been easier and quicker, I saw a sign to Rowleth Woods and decided to take the path by the river. It was a happy choice in a way; the woods were alive with birdsong and rabbits. I nearly stepped on two baby ducks on the path. I assumed they were Mandarin ducks and must have just jumped from the nest in a nearby tree and were making their way to the river. Pink Campion, Bugle, Marsh Marigold Forget-me-nots, Bluebells, Bird Cherry, Stitch Wort, Meadow Buttercup; Scharlie in her element; me leading the way and Scharlie and Bridget chatting away. They stopped

Rowleth Wood

to say hello to a couple of horses, one of which wanted to have its nose scratched. A young man in waders was casting in the stream for brown trout.

Beautiful stone arch bridges on the river and bank to protect the meadows from flooding. The river must get much higher sometimes because the debris in the trees is five or six feet above the current river level.

We reached Reeth and wandered through the housing estate to reach the marketplace, the broad open area in the centre of the village and found our B&B. the Manse. First, though I popped into Harkness Coaches to fix a taxi booking back to Keld to pick up the car.

Tea and cake in the garden and then a sunny drive back to Keld. The driver told me to go carefully on the way back on the narrow winding road. I enjoyed the drive in the evening sun with a window down and the wind in my hair, passing the lane I'd climbed out of Thwaite on up to Great Shunner Fell on the Pennine Way. I passed a turn to Askrigg and fancied exploring the lanes here. We had planned to come here last year on the motorbike but Covid intervened, and now I'm planning to sell it. I'd forgotten that I'd already booked dinner at the Buck Hotel a couple of weeks ago and Scharlie had double booked so I wandered over and cancelled one of the bookings.

We got there early and went into the restaurant, an octagonal extension in

Stepping stones across Barney Beck near confluence with Swale

what may have been the stable yard. We were served a nice bottle of wine and ordered. But they didn't have my first choice nor my second and there seemed to be some problem in the kitchen. We waited and waited. Finally the waitress came to apologise and to explain that they were short-staffed; the chef had called in sick and there was only one cook for both restaurant and bar meals. We were finally served at 9.30 but we'd been chatting happily if with increasing hunger pains. Soup was good but the main dishes were poor and Scharlie's mushroom burger consisted of a couple of bedraggled porcini mushrooms. The diffident young man in a tight black outfit came to settle up and asked if everything was all right in the usual formulaic way. It wasn't, I said calmly. Two hours late and poor main courses. Clearly something has gone very wrong in the kitchen and you didn't order the ingredients you needed, especially the fish and the mushrooms for Scharlie's burger and Bridget's risotto. Oh, he said and disappeared. We waited again and finally gave up and got our coats and went through to the bar to pay. They discounted Scharlie's burger.

The Manse Guest House Reeth (hosts Kim and Michael Gosschalk)

Day 9 Reeth to Richmond

Friday 28 May 2021 (9.6 miles)

A nice breakfast and I was away soon after nine, walking past the open market in the village green and down to the water meadows and along the river past two magnificent stone bridges. Then a gentle climb up to Marrick Priory where I stopped to take off my jacket and discovered I still had our room key in my pocket. I rang Scharlie. She and Michael, our host, were searching the room for it. She and Bridget came in the car and got it and I only had to wait a few minutes.

A climb up a broad grass path to Marrick village and then farmland to an isolated house, newly painted, called Ellers a good mile from the nearest road. Maybe they drive across the fields, I wondered. There is a steep road section down to Marske and it began to drizzle so I stopped at a covered stone seat let into the wall of Marske hall. The grounds extended on the other side of the road with an ornamental pond and classical folly. A heron landed as I watched,

Market Square Reeth

leaning on the gate. I went back to the stone bench and ate my lunch – a cheese sandwich and green apple.

From there I climbed the road, then through a style into lush pastures overlooking the Swale and dropped down to Paddy's bridge, a narrow footbridge over a beck. There was then a short ascent to Applegate Scar a limestone escarpment covered in ivy and vegetation and obviously not climbed or all the vegetation would have gone. There was a tall cairn in the form of a beautifully built cone. On the bridle path leading into Richmond I met another walker. He was in training for the coast-to-coast and plans to do it in a couple of weeks time. He said he was ex-military and retired from his current job which I later learnt was in the police. He told me he was writing a history of the 17th Lancers, his old regiment, from the time of the First World War to now.

I asked him why he hadn't gone back earlier. He had already told me that they had been at Balaclava. He said the early years were extensively documented but little had been written about the recent times. And most histories have focused on the officers and daring dos and he wanted to document the lives of ordinary soldiers. His aim was to write what he could find out about everyone who had ever served in the regiment. It's up to

Marrick Priory

Town Square Richmond

Fish and Chip supper, Castle Tavern Richmond

250,000 words, he said. Do you want to get it published? Yes of course, he said. I asked if he had a system and he said he used Excel to hold the basic information about each person and had paper files on each of them.

We left the road and strode out down the fields into Richmond. My digs were on the Reeth Road and quite soon after reaching the houses I realised I was there and hurriedly said goodbye. His military training kicked in and he seemed to straighten up to attention before he wished me luck, saying he was glad he'd met me.

Scharlie rang to say they were still in Richmond and having a great time visiting Easby Abbey. So they called in and we had a few minutes in the lounge in the B&B before they set off back to Leveret Croft. After they left rather than lie down, which part of me wanted to do, I set off into town. Richmond is delightful, with cobble streets and a great variety of building styles. I reached the main square and walked the narrow alleys near the castle, found the chip shop and sat eating fish, chips and mushy peas in the square. I got back to the digs before eight and fell into a deep sleep waking at 10 for an hour before going off again till breakfast time.

Pinfold House, Richmond, David and Tania

Day 10 Richmond to Danby Wiske

Saturday 29 May 2021 (16.0 miles)

Tanya, David's partner, served breakfast and was chatty and asked me about the trip. She has a strong accent and I guess she may be Polish. The coffee was good and eggs nicely cooked. I was going upstairs when she seemed to pounce on me from the kitchen. I assume she wanted paying but she was waving a card receipt. David explained that they took the money after the guest had stayed but they needed a further £5 for the lunch.

It was a beautiful clear morning, cool in the early morning light as I made my way down to the bridge over the Swale. The castle looks most formidable from the south. The way takes a series of interconnected paths and it's easy to follow the wrong one. I passed Easby Abbey, half a mile away. Then on across fields to Brompton-on-Swale then the bridge at Catterick and passed Scorton quarry pits with their danger signs. A man with a telescope and binoculars was watching the lakes. What have you seen, I asked. A pair of Shelduck, Plover and

Richmond Castle from the banks of the Swale

lots of Graylag Geese.

There is a stretch of road near Kipling Hall but luckily the broad verge had been mown and it was fairly easy walking. The hall was open and advertising tea and cake and I was tempted but continued. The gateway at Moorhouse Farm was a sea of slurry and difficult to negotiate and while most farmers leave a grassy edge to their fields this farmer and one or two others plough right to the edge that leaves a muddy, indefinite track.

The delightful green lane bounded by hedgerow on either side led to the road and Danby Wiske.

I stopped for lunch after Ladybank House and lay down on the grass and took off my boots. I was just dozing when I heard a noise on the other side of the hedge and a large black animal took fright and ran-off. It was most probably a dog though it might have been a badger.

There was a sign to the Coast-to-Coast tuck shop in Danby Wiske so I went and looked in at the brick shed. There was cake and flapjack, ice cream and icelollys, soft drinks and sweets; and an honesty box. A woman was working at a garden table and I asked if there was anywhere in the village where I could get a cup of tea. I'll make you one would you like a glass of water? I went back and selected a piece of almond cake. We got chatting. Her teenage daughter

Village pump, Bolton-on-Swale

Tilly has cerebral palsy and the family came here six months ago when her husband retired from the police. Vicky is a midwifery nurse in Tyneside. They have 7 acres and are enjoying settling in to country life. The hens came to say hello and she shooed them off. They have just bought an ancient tractor and her husband, Steven, was working on it with an old-boy in the barn.

My sister and brother-in-law went to Oxford; both from modest backgrounds, she said, and their son is trying, without success so far to get into Oxford. He went to Eton and I wonder with this current lot in Government if there is a prejudice against Etonians. I'd ban private education, I said. It's interesting the different attitudes to private education; it would save parents a lot of money, she said, .

Her husband a large man with a friendly smile, came over and asked if I'd like an ice lolly. He left us to continue chatting. My husband is planning to do the Coast-to-Coast in a few weeks with friends, but they're doing it in three stages, she said. I think that misses something about the whole experience of doing it in one. How far are you going today? I had wanted to get to Ingleby Cross, but that's a big step. Yes it's still long way. You can camp here if you like. That's very kind of you but I think I'll push on. I imagined that bivvying in their field might look a bit odd. She filled my water bottles and they felt heavy as I

Wooded paths, muddy after heavy rain last week

set off again.

Leaving the village a man with a gin and tonic was looking over his gate and said hello. He asked if I was doing the Coast-to-Coast and said he was impressed. At least the weather is much better today and it's flat, he said. It still seems tough, I said. Yes, and a bit boring with no views, just crossing fields, he said. Where will you stay tonight? I'll stop when I'm tired. If you're tired now you can stop in my field. Again I felt awkward and wanted to find a secluded spot.

A mile or so further on I found what I was looking for – a line of trees below Lazenby Grange on the grassy edge of a field with buttercups. It was six o'clock and I slept for an hour, then made a meal and got to bed just as the sun was setting below the trees.

Tuck Shop at Church Holme farm, Danby Wiske

Day 11 Danby Wiske to Clay Bank Top

Sunday 30 May 2021 (19.1 miles)

I woke with the light to a dawn chorus and dozed on for a couple of hours. There was a heavy dew and my sack was damp. I packed my things and had my breakfast and set off across the wet cornfield. The long fields and scattered farms blur one's memory. A startled pheasant shot out of the corn at my feet. A field already cut for hay. What in the dry would have been a delightful greenway between high hedges was a quaggy nightmare. A large flock of gulls and crows were feeding on a nearby newly mown field. This is horse country – the farms have stabling, parked horse-boxes and paddocks with eventing jumps . Rabbits running for cover and then diving into their burrows under the hedge line.

You have to cross the main railway line. I thought it was safe enough to stop and take photos looking down the track but just after I'd crossed a goods train went past. It seemed an endless slog but finally I reach the dual carriageway

Crossing the East Coast main line near Wray House

Ingleby Arncliffe water tower 1915

A most welcome coffee sitting outside at Joiners Cafe Ingleby Cross

of the A19 Thirsk Road and spot a gap and make a dash for the central reservation and then another dash for the safety of the far side.

In Ingleby Armscliff I stopped to rest on a bench in front of the water tower. I walked on to Ingleby Cross just down the road and found Joiners cafe was open and ordered a coffee. I sat outside and a man in a Discovery parked next to where I was sitting outside and left the engine running. I went over and asked him if he would be so kind as to turn his engine off. Why? Because I'm breathing the fumes. He sat saying nothing, but he switched off and I thanked him.

Arncliffe Hall, on the road that climbs the hill out of Ingleby Cross, is a beautifully symmetrical Palladian manor house of modest proportions – three stories of square honest soft red sandstone. Further up the road I met a lady on crutches out walking her Jack Russell terrier. She asked me if I was doing the Coast-to-Coast. She said she had lived here all her life. I fondly imagined in the Hall. It's a lovely spot, I said. Not so nice in the winter, she said.

There followed a rather tedious forest track that goes south towards Osmotherley to join the Cleveland Way. It's hard going so far in seemingly the wrong direction. The path steepens and finally reaches the northern edge of the moors. There are big ups and downs to get across the valleys and it's

Arncliffe Hall, Ingleby Cross 1753-54 Grade 1

frustrating losing all the height one has gained.

I reached Sugdale Beck and was glad I wasn't relying on it for water as the stream looked polluted. The route climbs Round Hill to Live Moor on a steep path with sandstone steps. I wanted to reach the cafe of Lord Stones before they closed but I stopped at a bench just before Hollin Hill for a quick break and a Trek bar. A chaffinch was sitting on the bench and let me get close before flying off into a nearby tree. I'm going quite well and making good time on the flagged path.

Finally I reached the steep descent to the road and the cafe. Disappointingly they aren't serving food. I ordered a pot of tea, a ginger beer and a large iced water together with chocolate and orange cake. Finding a bench I sat and relaxed in the afternoon sunshine. The shop is stocked with expensive luxury items but no bread or anything I can use to make a meal. Unfortunately what I thought was ham was bacon. You have lovely produce but nothing for someone doing the Coast-to-Coast to eat. You mean to make a meal? Yes, it all needs cooking. You're missing a trick; there will be lots of walkers coming through here. The cafe closed at four but there was a tap round the back and I filled my water bottles.

It was hard setting off again and there was a hill to climb to reach Kirby

Cleveland Way above Osmotherley

Scarth Wood Moor

Clain Wood

Carlton Moor boundary stone and summit cairn 408m

Welcome break at cafe at Lord Stones

Memorial to Alec Falconer, "Rambler"

Cream mare sniffing my toes

Bank and Cringle Moor, which I took slowly. Then a descent to grassy meadows before the next climb. A stone wall looked inviting so I sat and decided to stop here where the track to Bleak Hills crosses. My mother's house in Rainhill near St Helens I remembered was called Bleak Hill, a name I always associated with her unhappy childhood. It was sunny and warm and a marvellous evening. I unpacked and hung my damp sleeping bag and bivvi bag on the Cleveland Way sign, blew up my mattress and stretched out. I'd only been there a few minutes when two cart horses and a beautiful cream mare came over to investigate. The mare was fascinated by the smell of my sleeping bag and came closer to drop her head and chomp the grass between my legs. She was interested in my feet and it was strangely delightful feeling her warm exhalations on my toes and legs. An elderly gent descended the hill as I watched and stopped to chat. He asked if I planned to camp here. I said I planned to bivvi but I had wanted get to Clay Bank. That would be another two hours, he said, with a couple of climbs and a big descent. That's a big horse, he said.

Path up Hasty Bank, the last of the ascents before camping for the night

Wainstones, Hasty Bank

Bivvi site above Clay Bank Top on White Hill, Hasty Bank with view towards Roseberry Topping

After he left the mare began pushing under my mattress to get at the grass I was lying on and I wondered how well I would sleep with them nosing around me. So I changed my mind. I was feeling stronger after my rest and repacked in five minutes and was away.

I managed the next two hills fine, the second, White Hill has a rocky summit overlooking the Wain Stones. Then there was an easy stroll along Hasty Bank in the evening sunshine looking out for places to stop till just before the descent to Clay bank I found a promontory looking towards Roseberry Topping and stopped and made camp on a narrow sloping site with the prospect of sliding off in my slippery bivvi bag.

Misty cold and damp dawn

Day 12 Clay Bank Top to Glaisdale

Monday, 31 May (20.0 miles)

It was cold at dawn, with a chill breeze and a watery sun the size of the moon peeping through the thick mist. I lay till five and rousted myself out, pulling on my fleece, shorts and boots and packing quickly, hoping to stop at Clay Bank where it was more sheltered and perhaps have breakfast. The strong wind dropped on the descent but it was still cold at the road so I put on my anorak and over-trousers and set off up the fairly easy slope to the ridge. I passed two or three benches, dedicated to loved ones, and all of the same design by Taylor Bros of Pickering. Finally I reached the moor top and the mist cleared, with a strong inversion and a thick blanket of cloud hanging still in the valleys and over the plain to the west with the TV mast poking out of the fog at Bilsdale. Alarmed by my approach two hares leapt away, bounding over the heather. A

Benches I liked by Taylor Brothers of Pickering

Urra Moor and cloud inversion with Holme Moss Transmitter poking through the mist

Marker stones where path from Greenhow to Urra crosses Lyke Wake Walk

Breakfast at ordnance survey pillar on Round Hill, Urra Moor, highest point on Cleveland Hills

Hand stone, marking 'raodway' across Urra Moor

line of ancient stones marked an indefinite track running north south across the high moor.

At the top of Round Hill I left the track and climbed to the summit cairn and had my breakfast of muesli, savouring the dried cranberries. A man on a bike rode past on the track; he didn't turn to wave as I expected. The track follows the line of the disused railway that runs for miles along Blakey Ridge. It's flat but in a way that adds to its tediousness. A pair of curlews buzzed me, calling me away from their nest. Their alarm call changes as soon as I've moved on and they glide into land. Three grouse chicks skittering for cover in a ditch by the side of the track. The railway is embanked where it crosses dips. It must have brought shooting parties up onto the Moors as well as carrying stone and timber. There are dozens of disused lines here in North Yorkshire and the area must have been crisscrossed.

I heard cars and saw what I took to be the Lion Inn on the skyline but as I got near the track looked rough and all I could see was a brick shed and a stone wall and I assumed I must have been mistaken and carried on. Luckily I stopped to check the map and realised I should have climbed the rough track to the road. The pub didn't open till twelve, but I stopped to take off my boots and rest my feet in the garden anyway and decided to stay and read my book

Lion Inn, Blakey Ridge

until it opened. The waitress served me first and I ordered ham and cheese sandwich and a glass of fresh orange juice. Afterwards I climbed the tiny hill to get a photograph of the stone cross.

You then have to follow the road for 4-5 miles to get round the head of Rosedale and thus avoid dropping down into the valley. The original Wainwright route takes a path that cuts off the last bit of the loop but I didn't think it would save any time and it looked like it might be boggy in the bottom. I managed to walk on the grass verge so it wasn't too bad.

Where you fork right there is a splendid ancient cross but from here there were no grass verges and I had to walk on the road and my feet hurt. There was a bulbous stone cross where you fork left and continue to the bridle path sign to Glaisdale. You come to Trough House, an isolated shooting lodge with an interesting long stone bench outside. On Blakey Ridge the shoots have slate signs with the family names of Sykes, Blakey and many others.

There was another tedious stretch of road and then a stony track down Glaisdale Rigg. I don't know what I hate more, stony tracks or hard roads. It's a beautiful evening though, even if my feet hurt. I should have studied the map more carefully because I was horribly disillusioned to discover that the Armscliffe Arms, where I'm staying, is at Carr End, nearly 2 miles down the

Ralph Cross, Rosedale Head

Trough House, shooting lodge with distinctive trough in front of entrance

road. I got there finally and showered and dozed until Scharlie called. Then salmon and a pint and a chat with Simon who I'd seen earlier at the Lion Inn. He's in the building trade – mechanical and plumbing – and knew all about heat pumps. Covid has pushed him into handing in his notice. He disapproved of his firm's sloppy approach to health and safety and there lack of interest in doing a good job. He might go into training and has talked to people in Sheffield.

Day 13 Glaisdale to Robin Hoods Bay

Tuesday 1 June (18.3 miles)

I woke early, but breakfast wasn't till later. I was already packed so I read my book and went down to breakfast early and had juice and yogurt while I waited for the cooked breakfast I'd ordered. I was quickly away and making a good time along a delightful forest trail by the side of the River Esk. Then there was a section of road into Grosmont. It's a lovely day and I feel fit. I had just passed the level crossing when I heard the train whistle and went back to see a sensational black engine steaming up.

There is a brutally steep hill out of the village and I took it steadily. Simon and his friend from the Armscliffe Arms had passed me and were sitting by what I supposed was the shortcut left. I was lazy and didn't check my map and just followed them. It soon hit me that we had turned too early. They reasoned that there was a path that would cut out the first bit of road so we trudged

Beggar's Bridge Glaisdale

East Arnecliffe Wood

Steam train Grosmont North York Moors railway Society, Whitby to Pickering line

Falling Water, Littlebeck

The Hermitage Littlebeck, carved from a single sandstone boulder

across the moor. But we missed the path, so I headed for the summit of Black Brow to get a better view. We found our way and regained the road exactly at the gate to the Littlebeck path across the moor.

Littlebeck threads its way through bluebell woods. It's a gorgeous spot that has attracted lots of people on this sunny day. It seemed a long way by the side of the beck but I finally arrived at the top and turned to climb the road, luckily with a wide verge. The path across Sneaton Low Moor was boggy in places, then the final long moor of the walk over Graystone Hills.

There was a lovely shady lane that led to a long road section all the way into Hawsker. There is much too much road on the Coast-to-Coast, much more than on the Pennine Way, and the Coast-to-Coast feels more contrived and less of a logical route. The Pennine Way crosses the Pennines from side to side but always to gain or keep to high ground or to follow watershed. The Coast-to-Coast feels like Wainwright cleverly linked nice sections of bridleways and ancient trackways but the links weren't particularly elegant; maybe he did them by car.

After Hawkster you pass holiday camps of mobile homes laid out with military precision and the verges had just been shaved bald. Further on there was a delightful verge of wild flowers – Bluebells, Campion and Forget-me-

Northcliffe caravan park High Hawsker

Maw Wyke Hole and coastal path

Ness Point and coast guard station nearing end of the journey

nots, so much prettier and more beneficial.

Finally I reached the coastal path, with gulls wheeling over the cliffs, and headed south, dawdling because I was tired and because I wanted to savour the last mile or so. Maybe this is the last big walk I'll do; not sure I have the interest to do more, although Offa's Dyke appeals. So the walk started and finished with a cliff-walk with a sea to my left, starting in the rain and ending in warm bright sunshine. I checked in briefly at the B&B and then headed down to the Hard for ice cream and to dip my feet in the North Sea. I sat outside the Fish Box waiting for Scharlie who rang to say she had arrived and would walk down and meet me.

The following morning was sunny and warm and after breakfast we sauntered down to the sea. The tide was in and we traversed round to the beach. I'd waited to deposit my St Bees pebble with Scharlie and found a drilled shot hole in one of the rocks just big enough to drop the pebble into.

In the car on the way home by following single track moorland roads I showed Scharlie part of my route over the moors until we reached Ingleby Armscliffe and joined the A19 main road south.

Dipping my toes in the North Sea at Robin Hoods bay

Fish Box cafe

Scharlie tucking into fish and chips in the evening sunshine

Most of the pubs are still closed

Dropping the pebble carried from St Bees head into a shot hole in a rock

ITINERARY

Day	Date	Start	Finish	Km	Mile	Ht.	Accommodation
0	Wed 19-May	Leveret Croft	St Bees				Moorclose B&B
1	Thu 20-May	St Bees	Ennerdale Bridge	22.6	14.0	685	Thorntrees
2	Fri 21-May	Ennerdale Bridge	Rosthwaite	24.5	15.2	530	Gillercombe B&B
3	Sat 22-May	Rosthwaite	Glenridding	24.2	15.0	1035	Fairlight
4	Sun 23-May	Glenridding	Shap	25.1	15.6	762	New Ing Lodge
5	Mon 24-May	Shap	Sunbiggin Tarn	17.3	10.7	107	Camp
6	Tue 25-May	Sunbiggin Tarn	Kirkby Stephen	14.5	9.0	0	Jolly Farmers
7	Wed 26-May	Kirkby Stephen	Keld Lodge	19.3	12.0	515	Keld Lodge
8	Thu 27-May	Keld	Reeth	19.6	12.2	130	Manse
9	Fri 28-May	Reeth	Richmond	15.5	9.6	335	Pinfold House
10	Sat 29-May	Richmond	Danby Wiske	25.8	16.0	135	Bivi
11	Sun 30-May	Danby Wiske	Clay Bank Top	30.7	19.1	775	Bivi
12	Mon 31-May	White Hill	Glaisdale	32.2	20.0	310	Arncliffe Arms
13	Tue 01-Jun	Glaisdale	Robin Hoods Bay	29.4	18.3	500	North Ings
TOTAL				301	187	5819	

There is a slight discrepancy between my measurement of the distance covered 187 miles and the usually accepted distance 182 miles. I used a map wheel with 1:40,000 maps to measure the distance each day. Wikipedia puts the total at 182 miles (293km) Cicerone Guide by Terry Marsh gives 178 miles (286km). https://www.walkingenglishman.com/coast2coast.htm has 190 miles.1210161

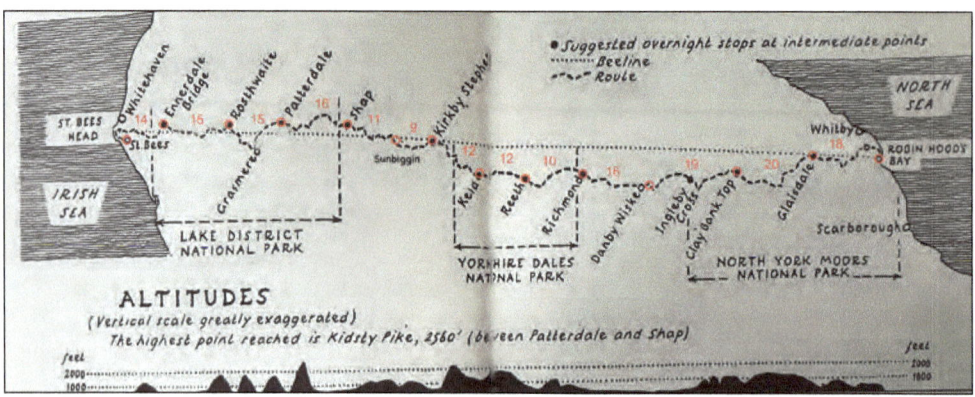

KIT LIST

Item	Make	Model	Notes	Quantity	Weight gm	Stars
Rucksack	Lightwave	U1	Excellent, durable but very light. Could do with larger side pockets	1	993	***
Tent	Nordisk	Telemark 2	Fantastic light tent, very waterproof. Attached extra guys for strong winds	1	950	***
Sleeping bag	RAB	Old Ascent 1100 equivalent	Warm but heavy	1	1,712	**
Mat	Thermarest	Prolite 3 ladies	Good, old so may be better options	1	620	**
Stove / pan	Jetboil		Excellent system; fast, light and packs small	1	326	***
Gaz	Primus		Good	1	180	***
Water canteen	Nalgene	48 oz	Excellent flexible fold up version, filled when lack of streams	1	1,750	***
Water bottle	Platyus		Good, works well	1	1,080	***
Knife	Gerber	Paraframe mini	Excellent, light and very sharpenable	1	55	***
Lighter	Torjet		Excellent, better than Bic	1	21	***
First aid kit			Good, added compeed, second skin, arnica.	1	123	***
Note book	Moleskin		I always use this make for my journals	1	111	***
Pens	Biro		Excellent	2	22	***
Phone	iPhone	12	Good battery life, excellent camera	1	75	***
Battery/cable	Anker	72 wh	Excellent	1	343	***
Sun glasses			Excellent cheap TK Max glasses	1	25	
Maps	Harvey	Coast to Coast West + East	Excellent, very accurate, durable and easy to use	2	46	***
Compass	Silva	with whistle	Excellent, very practical, have always used Silva	1	42	***
Headtorch	Petzl	e+lite	Unnecessary	1	26	***
Debit card			Essential	1	1	
Dry bags	Sea to Summit	Assorted	Excellent, durable and completely waterproof	5	310	***
Duvet	Marmot	Chaleco	Excellent, down very warm	1	412	***
Walking poles	Black Diamond	Distance flz	Excellent, light and well balanced	2	384	***
Sandals	Clogs		Useful in camp for tired feet and for getting water from streams	1	296	**
Overtousers	Berghaus	Gortex Paclite	Used	1	192	***
TOTAL KIT					**10,095**	
Water purification	Oasis		Necessary if wild camping and getting water from streams	6	17	***
Oats/dried fruit			I mixed jumbo oats with assorted nuts and dried fruit - raisins, apple and bar	1	500	***
Freeze dried pack	Expedition		Excellent, light and tasty, especially fish and potato and Thai chicken and veg	2	400	**
Oat bars	Trek		Excellent energy giving snack	4	96	***
Tea bags	Yorkshire		10 Excellent	1	34	***
Sugar		17/07/202117/07/202117/07/2021		1	15	
Salt and pepper				1	15	
Lip salve	Soltan	factor 30		1	7	
Sun cream	Nivea	Sun 30		1	45	
Toothpaste	Colgate			1	15	
Toothbrush	CuraProx			1	10	
Soap			Fag end of a used bar	1	17	
Shampoo			Used once	1	14	
Towel	Go			1	42	
Toilet paper			End of a roll	1	30	
Contact lenses				1	12	
Spectacles				1	70	
Eye drops				1	9	
TOTAL FOOD					**1,338**	
Boots	Meindl	Bhutan	Excellent, especially for wider feet	1	1,964	***
Gaiters	Sea to Summit		Good, light	1	110	**
Anorak	Arcteryx	Alpha SV	Orange	1	506	***
Fleece	Berghaus		Windproof with hood	1	518	***
Overtousers	Berghaus	Gortex Paclite	Used	1	192	***
Cap	North face		Excellent, old friend	1	86	***
Pants	Kühl		Excellent, fit well and good pockets	1	351	***
Shorts	Kühl		Excellent, fit well and good pockets	1	299	***
T shirts	Adidas		Excellent, stayed looking smart	1	150	***
Inner socks	Coolmax		These are very old and I should have bought new	2	104	**
Outer socks	Bridgedale		Excellent, very comfortable	2	0	***
Underpants	M&S			2	46	
Belt	Jukmo	Ratchet belt	Essential, because you loose weight (6-7 kilos).	1	25	
TOTAL WORN					**4,351**	

Kinder Training Walk

Monday 19 April - Tuesday 20 2021

A splendid day; bright sun, blue sky and a cool breeze. Scharlie dropped me on the lane to Fullwood Stile Farm. I struggled a bit on the pull up to Wooler Knoll. Birdsong and clear light. I kept stopping to admire the view and fix the geography in my mind: the slope up to Lose Hill and whether I could see an obvious way down. Skylarks as I reached the Roman road from Win Hill. A few people about, everyone happy with the glorious weather. There was someone at Hope Cross and since I wanted to take a photo I went into the Scots Pine wood through a gate and found a fallen log to sit on in the shade.

An easy pull up the grassy field to Crookstone Barn where you have to climb the locked gate then Crookstone Hill to the knoll where the path I wanted went right to the end of the plateau before curving round to head west past Madwoman's Stones on the skyline. Then on to Blackdon Edge and

Setting off up Win Hill from Fullwood Road End

Hope Cross (1737), Roman road where Hope to Ashop way crosses Edale to Derwent

Crookstone Barn

Blackdon Clough where I stopped for lunch. The water was brackish with peat and slow-moving but I filled up anyway, reasoning that this might be my only chance. It was; Fairbrook, the other main water course, was dry. Sand lizards, russet and green, skittered across the path and disappeared quickly in the grass.

Along Seal Edge, that Scharlie and I climbed directly from the road one winter in deep snow, and on to Fairbrook Naze. The path is crossed by boulders and peat hags and isn't easy. I came the opposite way last year with an easterly gale blowing in my face. Today is easier.

I could see over into the Derwent Valley. The Salt Cellar rocks on Derwent Edge, Hagg Side, the Snake road and Alport Castles. It's fascinating following the lie of the land and imagining routes.

I'm a bit doddery and have to take care not to hurt myself. It would be easy to twist an ankle on one of the drops off a boulder or trip and go headfirst and do more damage.

Finally I reached the end of the plateau having traversed the full length of the northern edge. and joined the Pennine Way – the stretch I did last year in a bitter storm. Just before Kinder Downfall I stopped to chat to a strapping young man with an enormous pack. I asked if he was doing the Pennine Way.

Crookstone Hill and Knott

Stone near Blackden Edge

Looking east along northern edge of the Kinder plateau from Fairbrook Naze

Face stones The Edge, Kinder

Kinder Gates

I'd like to, he said. I'm just starting. This will be my first night wild camping. I have to carry water and food for both me and my dog – a gorgeous ginger spaniel puppy. I stopped at the Downfall. Not a lot of water, it's been dry for while, but enough of a flow to fill my canteens.

I headed into the plateau towards Kinder Gates., obvious when I reach them .and found a soft sheltered spot to bivvi. I was writing my journal when I heard noises coming from the moor behind me. Two youths appeared, their noses glued to the maps on their phones. They hurried past looking nervous with the usual South Yorkshire greeting of Alright then! They disappeared along the main track south. I got out my things and made my bed. It looked inviting so I crawled in and fished out the stove and food. To my dismay I couldn't find the lighter. I must have left it on the bed at home when I was packing. So I poured cold water into the freeze-dried scrambled egg and left it for half an hour to rehydrate. Pity about the hot drink.

There was a cold breeze on my face that kept me awake, so I zipped up the bivvi bag leaving an opening to breathe. I had my duvet jacket as a pillow and felt snug. But it got very cold in the night and I woke to a starry sky and curlew calling in the dark. There was a glow from Manchester and Sheffield like two dawn lights. I fell asleep again and woke to a crackling of ice on the bivvi

Bivvi just beyond Kinder Gates

bag, a damp sleeping bag and cold knees. The water in the two water bottles was frozen. I lay for a moment watching the many aircraft contrails and planes heading from Manchester or further north. Covid hasn't stopped them flying like it did last year.

It took only ten minutes to pull on my boots and set off. The path was clear at first, following the watercourse but it disappeared in a water-filled defile where the footprints disapeared. I cast back to see if I'd gone wrong and then climbed the bank to get a better view. I got out the compass and set it to the map and struck off on a vague line across the moor. It was difficult, as I had to keep crossing minor watercourses, dropping down into boggy ground and having to scramble back up the opposite bank. I was heading for the rocks I could see on the skyline and knew I would eventually hit the southern edge of the plateau if I kept going. Finally I saw a path and made for it. The path must have followed the stream after all. I reached Crowden Clough and cut across to avoid losing height.

I stopped for breakfast on some pretty rocks. The sun was warm. as I started off again. Emerald green beetles flitting on the path and a pair of curlews landing on their nest in the heather below. I love their bubbling call and look forward to it each year as a sign of hope and joy. A solitary golden plover and

Top of Kinder Downfall

a raven on a glide path south.

I've been this way along the Edge before, but it seems further today. I finally reach Crookstone Hill and then the barn. It looks like a holiday home – lots of orange gas cylinders and Velux windows lighting the top story.

It seems a long way along the Roman Road climbing to Win Hill while it's such a doddle going the opposite way. Lots of people now, all friendly when I say hi. A scramble to the top and a welcome rest and an oat bar for lunch. Then it's the gentle walk down, with sore feet and a rest on a bench in Thornhill to write my notes before carrying on to John's to get a lift from Scharlie.

The song of the walk was "For those in peril on the sea". It must have been sung at Prince Philip's funeral. I watched Master and Commander again the other night. Maybe I'll download a Patrick O'Brian audiobook for the Coast-to-Coast. Just now I feel to old to embark on such a long walk.

Win Hill summit and Ladybower reservoir

Kinder Downfall

www.ingramcontent.com/pod-product-compliance
Lightning Source LLC
Chambersburg PA
CBHW041612220426
43669CB00001B/11